**United States Department of Agriculture**

I0467366

# Economic Research Service
www.ers.usda.gov

Access this report online:

www.ers.usda.gov/publications/eib-economic-information-bulletin/eib-123.aspx

Download the charts contained in this report:

- Go to the report's index page www.ers.usda.gov/publications/ eib-economic-information-bulletin/eib123.aspx
- Click on the bulleted item "Download eib123.zip"
- Open the chart you want, then save it to your computer

Recommended citation format for this publication:

Newton, Doris J. *Working the Land With 10 Acres: Small Acreage Farming in the United States, EIB-123*, U.S. Department of Agriculture, Economic Research Service, April 2014.

Cover image: Shutterstock.

Use of commercial and trade names does not imply approval or constitute endorsement by USDA.

The U.S. Department of Agriculture (USDA) prohibits discrimination in all its programs and activities on the basis of race, color, national origin, age, disability, and, where applicable, sex, marital status, familial status, parental status, religion, sexual orientation, genetic information, political beliefs, reprisal, or because all or a part of an individual's income is derived from any public assistance program. (Not all prohibited bases apply to all programs.) Persons with disabilities who require alternative means for communication of program information (Braille, large print, audiotape, etc.) should contact USDA's TARGET Center at (202) 720-2600 (voice and TDD).

To file a complaint of discrimination write to USDA, Director, Office of Civil Rights, 1400 Independence Avenue, S.W., Washington, D.C. 20250-9410 or call (800) 795-3272 (voice) or (202) 720-6382 (TDD). USDA is an equal opportunity provider and employer.

# Contents

Summary . . . . . . . . . . . . . . . . . . . . . . . . . . . . . . . . . . . . . . . . . . . . . . . . . . . . . . . . . . . . . . . . . . . .ii

Introduction . . . . . . . . . . . . . . . . . . . . . . . . . . . . . . . . . . . . . . . . . . . . . . . . . . . . . . . . . . . . . . . . .1

Farm Characteristics: General and Small Acreage Farms . . . . . . . . . . . . . . . . . . . . . . . . .2

    The Small Acreage Farm Landscape . . . . . . . . . . . . . . . . . . . . . . . . . . . . . . . . . . . .3
    Small Acreage Farm Sales . . . . . . . . . . . . . . . . . . . . . . . . . . . . . . . . . . . . . . . . . .6
    Acres Operated by Small Acreage Farmers . . . . . . . . . . . . . . . . . . . . . . . . . . . . . .8
    Farm Product Specializations and Sales of Small Acreage Farms . . . . . . . . . . . . . . . . .8

Top-Ranking Small Acreage Farm Product Specializations by Sales Class . . . . . . . . . . . . . . .10
    Small Acreage Farm Production and Farm Sector Changes . . . . . . . . . . . . . . . . . . . . .13

Small Acreage Farm Financial Performance . . . . . . . . . . . . . . . . . . . . . . . . . . . . . . . . . . .15

Small Acreage Farm Operator Household Income . . . . . . . . . . . . . . . . . . . . . . . . . . . . . . .18

Conclusions and Implications . . . . . . . . . . . . . . . . . . . . . . . . . . . . . . . . . . . . . . . . . . . . .20

References . . . . . . . . . . . . . . . . . . . . . . . . . . . . . . . . . . . . . . . . . . . . . . . . . . . . . . . . . .21

Appendix . . . . . . . . . . . . . . . . . . . . . . . . . . . . . . . . . . . . . . . . . . . . . . . . . . . . . . . . . . .24

United States Department of Agriculture

**Economic Research Service**

Economic Information Bulletin Number 123

April 2014

# Working the Land With 10 Acres: Small Acreage Farming in the United States

Doris J. Newton

## Abstract

According to the U.S. Census of Agriculture, 294,000 farms operated on 10 or fewer acres in 2007. While most small acreage (SA) operations did very little farming, approximately 50,000 SA farms had gross sales of $10,000 or more in 2007; 3,600 reported grossing $500,000 or more. Thus, a limited land base does not necessarily translate into low sales. This report focuses on SA farms, especially those grossing $10,000 or more in a given year, and examines such characteristics as production strategies, types of products, sales, household income, and financial performance. The 46,000 SA farms with sales between $10,000 and $500,000 in 2007 were primarily active in floriculture, tree nurseries, and fruits and vegetables, while the 3,600 SA farms with at least $500,000 in sales were primarily active in confined livestock production. SA farms produce only small amounts of field crops, such as wheat, corn, or cotton, which require larger amounts of land.

## Keywords

small acreage farming, farm structure, farm financial performance, farm operator household income, 10 acres or less, women farmers, women principal and secondary operators, small acreage farm characteristics, small farms

## Acknowledgments

The author thanks the following individuals for their thoughtful reviews: Jeremy Weber, Robert Hoppe, James M. Harris, Keithly Jones, Christopher Davis, Mildred Haley, Sun Ling Wang, James MacDonald, Patrick Sullivan, and Marca Weinberg of U.S. Department of Agriculture (USDA), Economic Research Service (ERS); Denis Ebodaghe, USDA, National Institute of Food and Agriculture; Susan Cocciarelli, Michigan State University; and an anonymous reviewer. The author also thanks John Weber and Curtia Taylor for editorial and design assistance.

**USDA**

**United States Department of Agriculture**

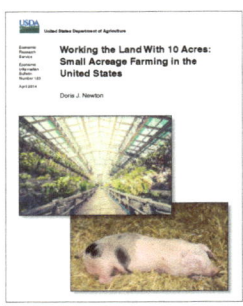

Find the full report at *www.ers.usda. gov/publications/eib-economic-information-bulletin/eib-123.aspx*

# Working the Land With 10 Acres: Small Acreage Farming in the United States

Doris J. Newton

## What Is the Issue?

Roughly 13 percent of U.S. farms (294,000) operated on 10 acres or less in 2007, and while most of these small acreage (SA) farms generated very little, if any, farm production, some managed to attain sizeable sales despite their limited land base. Given strong and growing empirical evidence that larger farms are more efficient at producing most farm products, what factors account for the apparent continuing financial viability of some small acreage farms? This report looks at small acreage farms having gross sales of $10,000 or more in a given year to better understand the product choices and strategies used by small acreage farms that appear to be operating profitably.

## What Did the Study Find?

**Almost one-sixth of all U.S. farms in 2007 were SA farms with 10 or fewer acres**. These operations controlled approximately 1.7 million acres of farmland (only 0.18 percent of the 922.1 million total acres of U.S. farmland in 2007). However, total sales of all SA farms were approximately $9 billion in 2007, or 3 percent of total U.S. farm sales.

**Most SA farms in 2007 produced very little, if any, farm products; yet, 17 percent of SA farms (50,000) had gross sales of at least $10,000.** Approximately 122,000 operations, or 42 percent of all SA farms, reported sales under $1,000 in 2007, while 41 percent reported sales between $1,000 and just under $10,000.

**Small acreage does not necessarily mean small sales**. Over 30,000 SA farms had sales between $10,000 and $50,000 in 2007, while 6,000 SA farms grossed over $250,000 and 3,600 had sales of at least $500,000. These farms tended to specialize in a single stage of the production process when raising livestock, or they produced high-value crops. They produced very little or no field crops, which require large acreages.

**Product specializations varied with the size of the farm.** The 3,600 farms in the largest SA sales class, at least $500,000 in sales in 2007, consisted primarily of confined hog and poultry operations. But the 46,000 farms with sales between $10,000 and $500,000 in 2007 focused primarily on high-value crops like floriculture, tree nurseries, orchards, and vegetables.

ERS is a primary source of economic research and analysis from the U.S. Department of Agriculture, providing timely information on economic and policy issues related to agriculture, food, the environment, and rural America.

**Small acreage (SA) farms and sales share by product specialization group, 2007**

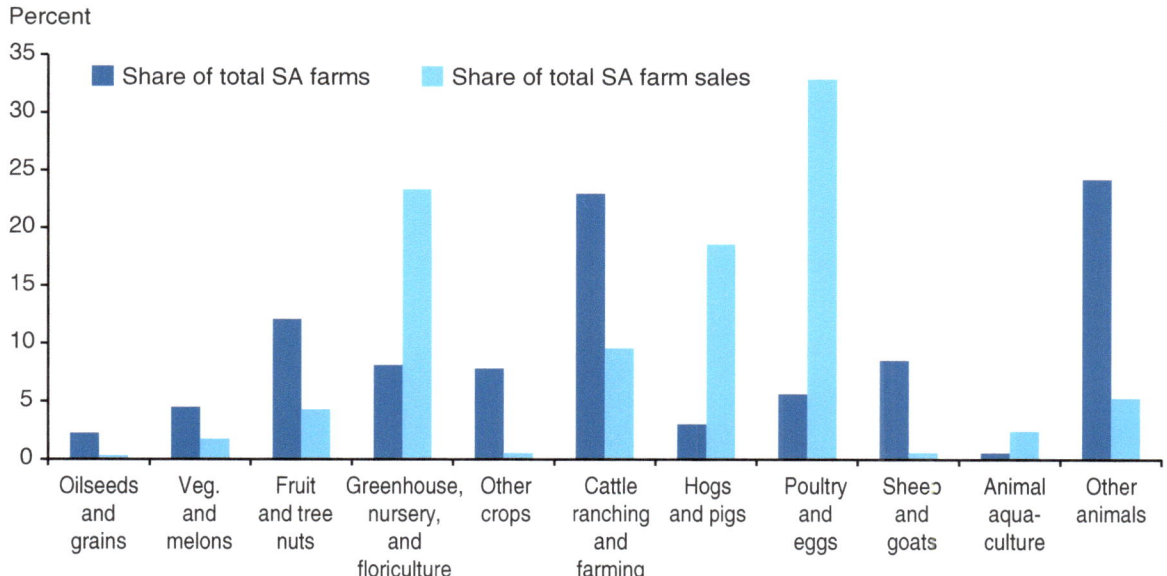

Sources: USDA, Economic Research Service using data from U.S. Census of Agriculture, 2007, and North American Industry Classification System.

**Most SA farms with sales greater than $10,000 in 2007 had positive net farm income**. The majority of SA farms with sales greater than $10,000 in 2007 realized gross income in excess of cash expenses, and the share with positive returns increased with sales class, except for farms with sales of at least $500,000. Cash expenses include the expense of hired labor but do not account for family-provided labor.

**Rates of return on equity for SA farms varied widely among sales classes**. ERS estimates of the rate of return on equity account for the costs of family-provided labor. Farms with sales of less than $100,000 in 2007 had negative rates of return, while farms with sales of $100,000 or more had positive rates of return.

**The share of women principal operators is higher for SA farms than for all farms.** Women were principal operators of 24 percent of all SA farms in 2007, compared with 14 percent of all farms. They were the principal operator on 19 percent of SA farms with sales of $10,000 or more, compared with 8 percent of all farms with sales that high.

## How Was the Study Conducted?

This report uses data from both the 2007 U.S. Census of Agriculture and USDA's 2007 Agricultural Resource Management Survey (ARMS) to examine the socioeconomic characteristics of the farming and ranching population whose production is on 10 acres or less. Every 5 years, the agricultural census collects information from farm operators on acres operated, product sales and volumes, operator characteristics, and farm finances. The 2007 census contains the latest available data on all farms at the time this research was completed, and it provides comprehensive details on production by SA farms. ARMS, an annual survey sponsored by USDA's Economic Research Service and National Agricultural Statistics Service, generates a representative national sample of 20,000-22,000 farms and provides additional farm and farm household financial information that is not collected in the census.

# Working the Land With 10 Acres: Small Acreage Farming in the United States

Doris J. Newton

## Introduction

Is it possible to successfully operate a farm on 10 acres or less? According to the U.S. Census of Agriculture, roughly 294,000 U.S. farms reported operating on 10 acres or less in 2007, the latest year for which data were available for this analysis. For purposes of this report, these farms are referred to as small acreage (SA) farms.

USDA defines a farm as any place from which $1,000 or more of agricultural products (crops and livestock) were produced or sold or normally would have been sold during the year under consideration. USDA's definition does not specify a minimum amount of acreage needed to qualify as a farm, but local government zoning ordinances and State farm support programs may implicitly or explicitly target farms based on the amount of farmland they operate. And for many individuals, a "small farm" may be defined more by the physical size of the operation rather than its financial status. While the amount of crops and livestock that can be produced is a function of the amount of land available to produce it on, the relationship depends on the type of product and choice of farming practices applied. Most SA farms generate very little, if any, farm production in a given year. However, based on the Census of Agriculture, 50,000 SA farms reported gross sales of at least $10,000 in 2007, and 3,600 reported sales of $500,000 or more. This report examines the characteristics of SA farms and the operators and households running them, with a particular focus on SA farms with gross sales of $10,000 or more in a given year.

USDA's Economic Research Service (ERS) has ongoing research that focuses on farm viability. In recent years, ERS has reported on the growing consolidation of production on larger farming operations and the economies of size pushing that trend (MacDonald et al., 2013; O'Donoghue et al., 2011), the aging farm population and trends in numbers of young, beginning farmers (Ahearn, 2013), and the role that small (sales) farms play in the agricultural sector (Hoppe et al., 2010). This report seeks to further this research by examining the role that small acreage farms play in agricultural production, specifically looking at farms that reported having operated on 10 or fewer acres of total farmland devoted to crop and livestock production in 2007. Increasing farmland prices in recent decades (Nickerson et al., 2012) have raised the cost of owning and renting a farm of any appreciable size, meaning some beginning farmers with limited access to land and capital may need to start small. At the same time, farm business viability is a function of production and sales, putting pressure on beginning farmers who want to make farming their primary occupation to find ways of increasing production. This report explores how some SA farm operators have successfully managed their farming business on a limited land base.

# Farm Characteristics: General and Small Acreage Farms

Over the last three decades, the size distribution of U.S. farms has changed significantly. Whether farm size is measured by sales or acreage, there has been an increase in the number of smaller and larger farms and a corresponding decline in midsized farms. Production has shifted steadily from midsized to larger farms. Between 1982 and 2007, the number of farms with less than $10,000 in sales (measured in 2007 dollars) in a given year and those with $250,000 or more increased while the number of farms in the middle—those with annual sales between $10,000 and $250,000— declined (table 1).[1]

Like sales, acreage has also shifted over time. Between 1982 and 2007, the number of farms with less than 50 acres and the number with more than 2,000 acres increased, while the numbers of farms in all intermediate classes declined. The numbers of farms with 50 to 179 acres and 500 to 999 acres declined roughly 2 percent or more over the period. Among all farm size classes, the largest decline was in farms that had 180 to 499 acres (table 2).

Several factors contributed to this general shift in farm size distribution. Large farms have better financial performance, on average, than small farms (Hoppe et al, 2010; MacDonald et al., 2013). This provides a strong incentive for farms to become larger and for production to shift to larger farms. Technological advances have increased farm productivity (O'Donoghue et al., 2011; Fuglie et al., 2007). Farms have benefited from productivity-enhancing technologies, such as more efficient

Table 1
**Distribution of U.S. farms and farm sales by sales class**

| | Number of farms | | Market value of sales (billion 2007 $) | |
|---|---|---|---|---|
| | 1982 | 2007 | 1982 | 2007 |
| Total | 2,240,976 | 2,204,793 | 189.1 | 297.2 |
| | *Farms and sales distribution by sales class (percent)* | | | |
| Sales class (2007 $) | | | | |
| Less than 10,000 | 42.6 | 59.8 | 1.8 | 0.9 |
| 10,000-249,999 | 50.8 | 30.7 | 40.8 | 14.2 |
| 250,000-999,999 | 5.9 | 7 | 30 | 25.7 |
| 1,000,000 or more | 0.7 | 2.5 | 27.4 | 59.2 |
| Total | 100 | 100 | 100 | 100 |

Note: Dollar figures have been adjusted for inflation so farms are categorized by sales measured in 2007 dollars.
Source: USDA, Economic Research Service using data from U.S. Census of Agriculture, 1982 and 2007.

---

[1]The adjustment for inflation is done because farm prices received have risen over time, so a farm with the same quantity of production would have higher sales in 2007 than in 1982 when measured in nominal (current) dollars. The inflation adjustment aims to correct for price changes so that we measure changes in real sales growth over time. According to the Producer Price Index for Farm Products, farm prices rose by 43 percent between 1982 and 2007.

Table 2
**Distribution of U.S. farms by acreage size**

| | Number of farms | | Percent change |
|---|---|---|---|
| | 1982 | 2007 | |
| Farms by size (acres): | | | |
| 1 to 9 | 187,665 | 232,849 | 2.2 |
| 10 to 49 | 449,252 | 620,283 | 8.1 |
| 50 to 179 | 711,652 | 660,530 | -1.8 |
| 180 to 499 | 526,510 | 368,368 | -6.8 |
| 500 to 999 | 203,925 | 149,713 | -2.3 |
| 1,000 to 1,999 | 97,395 | 92,656 | -0.1 |
| 2,000 or more | 64,577 | 80,393 | 0.8 |
| Total farms | 2,240,976 | 2,204,792 | |

Source: USDA, Economic Research Service using data from U.S. Census of Agriculture, 1982 and 2007.

farm machinery and advanced scientific disease and pest control, and more efficient use of productive resources, such as allowed by the use of production contracts. Scientific and organizational improvements enable farms to manage more acres and animals effectively.

At the same time, the number of very small farms, those with less than $10,000 in annual sales and/or with fewer than 70 acres of farmland, is increasing (Hoppe and Banker, 2010). A growing number of people who prefer a rural lifestyle have evidently found ways of acting on their preferences, including acquiring ownership of (or otherwise controlling) small amounts of cropland or livestock. However, the trend also reflects two methodological elements of farm surveys, which contribute to the increasing number of small farms as reported in the 2007 Census of Agriculture.

First, the farm definition, set at $1,000 in annual farm sales in 1975, is not adjusted for inflation, so more very small operations qualify as farms over time as commodity prices rise (see box "What Is a Farm?"). The Producer Price Index for Farm Products increased by 86 percent between 1975 and 2007. An operation that had $600 in sales in 1975 would not be defined as a farm in that year, but commodity price inflation would have boosted that same place over $1,000 in sales by 2007, qualifying it as a farm that year.

Second, the National Agricultural Statistics Service (NASS), USDA's primary data collection agency, has made substantial efforts in recent years to improve its coverage of small farms, and success in this endeavor has led to increasing numbers of small farms in its counts (NASS, 2011). NASS prepared for the 2007 Census of Agriculture by partnering with community-based organizations and producer groups to improve survey responses from smaller sales farms, including minority farms.

## The Small Acreage Farm Landscape

Farming does not always require much land to generate significant sales. Some farms operate on few acres yet have substantial sales. Almost one-sixth of all U.S. farms in 2007 were small acreage farms with 10 or fewer acres (table 3). As a group, SA farms controlled approximately 1.7 million

## What Is a Farm?

USDA defines farms very broadly in its statistical programs. Since 1850, when minimum criteria defining a farm for census purposes were first established, the farm definition has changed nine times as the Nation has grown. A farm is currently defined, for statistical purposes, as any place from which $1,000 or more of agricultural products (crops and livestock) were produced or sold or normally would have been sold during the year under consideration. This definition has been in place since August 1975—by joint agreement between USDA, the Office of Management and Budget, and the Bureau of the Census—and the per year sales amount has not been adjusted for inflation. According to the most recently available (2007) Census of Agriculture, just over 2.2 million farms operate in the United States. Approximately 689,000 farms (31.3 percent) sold less than $1,000 of agricultural products in 2007. These operations were defined as farms, even with sales under $1,000, because they received government farm program payments sufficient to put them over the sales threshold, or because they had cropland or livestock assets sufficient to generate sales of $1,000 had the farms produced and sold commodities from those assets.[1]

---

[1] If a place does not have $1,000 in sales, a "point system" assigns values for acres of various crops and head of various livestock species to estimate a normal level of sales. Point farms are farms with fewer than $1,000 in annual sales but with points worth at least $1,000. Point farms tend to be very small. Some, however, may normally have large sales but experience low sales in a particular year due to bad weather, disease, or other factors. Both the Agricultural Resource Management Survey (ARMS) and the Census of Agriculture use the point system to help identify farms meeting the current definition.

Table 3
**General characteristics of small acreage (SA) farms compared to all U.S. farms, 2007***

|  | All SA farms | Share of SA totals having $10,000 or more in sales | All U.S. farms | SA share of U.S. totals |
|---|---|---|---|---|
|  |  | *Percent* |  | *Percent* |
| Number of farms | 294,000 | 17 | 2,204,792 | 13 |
| Acreage (millions) | 1.7 | 16 | 922.1 | 0.18 |
| Sales ($ billions) | 8.9 | 95 | 297 | 3 |

*One-fifth of SA farms had gross annual sales of $10,000 or more and accounted for 95 percent of SA sales in 2007.
Source: USDA, Economic Research Service using data from U.S. Census of Agriculture, 2007..

acres of farmland (0.18 percent of the 922.1 million total acres of U.S. farmland in 2007). However, total sales of all SA farm operations were approximately $9 billion in 2007, or 3 percent of total U.S. farm sales.

Who are SA farmers? Not surprising, the majority (77 percent) of SA principal operators in 2007 were men (fig. 1). This finding is consistent with the distribution of farm operators in general, where men were the majority (86 percent). The share of women operators, however, was larger for SA farms than for all farms (fig. 2; see box "Women-Operated Small Acreage Farms").

Farmers in the United States are aging. The average farmer's age in 2007 was 57 years, and a quarter of all farmers were age 65 or older. SA farmers were slightly younger than the average age. Most SA farmers were age 45 or older, though 22 percent were age 65 or older—similar to the shares

Figure 1

**Small acreage (SA) and all farms with sales of $10,000 or more in 2007, by gender of principal operator**

Percent of farms

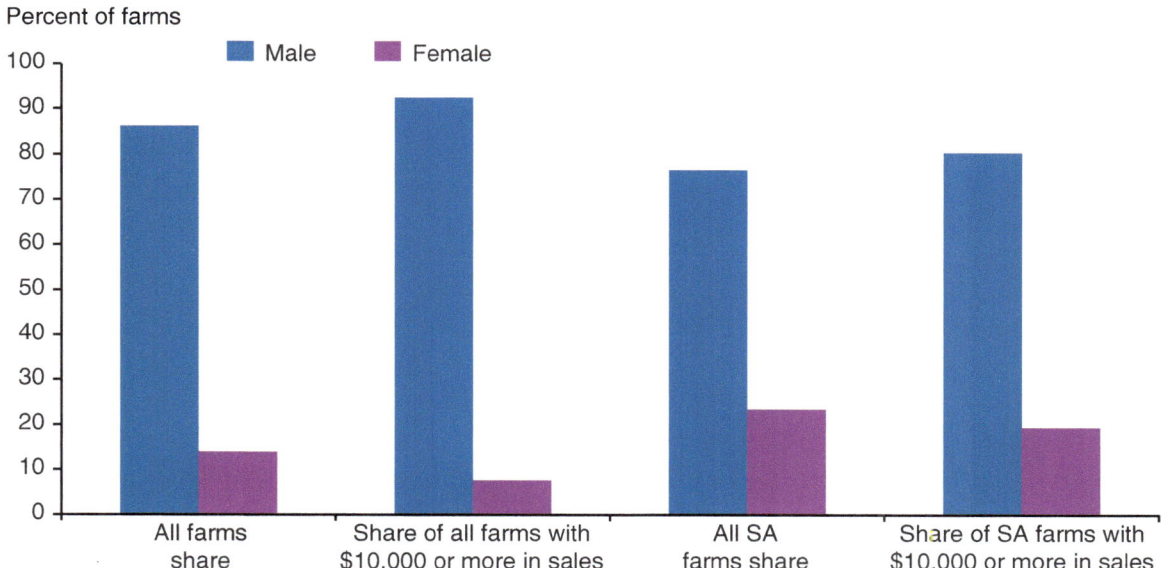

Source: USDA, Economic Research Service using data from U.S. Census of Agriculture, 2007.

Figure 2

**Small acreage (SA) and all farms with $10,000 or more in sales in 2007, by gender and with count of women principal and secondary operators combined**

Percent of farms

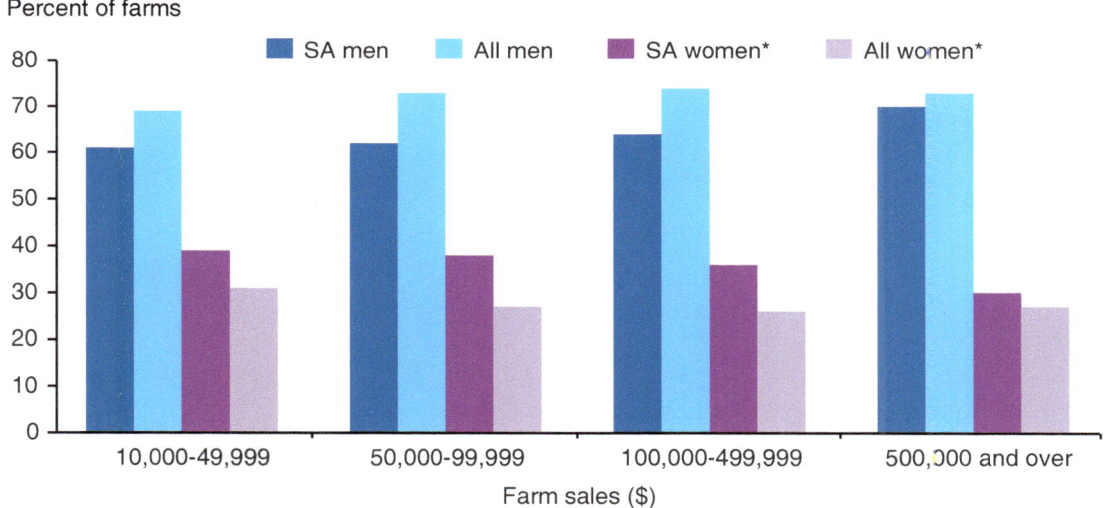

Farm sales ($)

*Includes women counted as principal and secondary farm operators, only. Census counts for secondary men and all third operators not included.
Farms with $10,000 or more in sales: SA men count = 39,567; SA women count = 24,329. All men count = 818,591; All women count = 330,157
Source: USDA, Economic Research Service using data from U.S. Census of Agriculture, 2007.

## Women-Operated Small Acreage Farms

Women are much more likely to be principal operators of small acreage (SA) farms than all farms combined (see figure 1 on page 5). In both the Census of Agriculture and USDA's Agricultural Resource Management Survey (sponsored by ERS and the National Agricultural Statistics Service, or NASS), information is collected on the person identified as the principal farm operator. NASS defines a *principal operator* as the person primarily responsible for the onsite, day-to-day operation of the farm or ranch business. This person could be an owner, hired manager, cash tenant, share tenant, and/or a partner.

Data by gender for principal farm operators was first collected in the 1978 Census of Agriculture. And since the 2002 Census of Agriculture, NASS has also collected data on up to three *operators* per farm, recognizing that in some cases farming responsibility is shared even though the second and third parties may not be responsible for day-to-day farm operations. Women farmers play a critical role in many farm operations. Most women farmers work with their husbands to help operate the farm. However, some women are principal farm operators. Unless otherwise indicated, this report focuses on the characteristics of the *principal* operator. Because women are often classified as secondary operators, secondary women farm operators are added to the total count of principal women farm operators as part of the analyses.

Women were principal operators of 24 percent of all SA farms in 2007, compared with 14 percent of all farms. They were the principal operator on 19 percent of SA farms with sales of $10,000 or more, compared with 8 percent of all similar sales farms. When principal and secondary women farm operators are counted, women-operated farms accounted for 58 percent of all SA farms in 2007 and 28 percent of all farms in general. Women-operated farms also accounted for 38 percent of all SA farms with sales of $10,000 or more in 2007 and 29 percent of all similar sales farms.

In every sales class, there were higher shares of women farm operators on SA farms with $10,000 or more sales than on all similar sales farms (see figure 2 on page 5). Most women operators of SA farms were in the lowest referenced sales class ($10,000-49,999). Similar to all SA farms, women-operated SA farms tended to produce specialty crops such as vegetables, fruit, tree nuts, and floriculture and raise beef cattle and other livestock such as horses, goats, and sheep.

for the general farm population (figs. 3 and 4). Among all principal SA farm operators, similar shares of men (25 percent) and women (21 percent) reported being retired.

Since access to land is important in farming, farm tenure—how land is held—is a major issue. The majority of SA farm operators in 2007 were full owners (90 percent), while about 4 percent indicated that they were part owners, owning part of the land they operate and renting the rest. The remaining SA farmers were renters.

## Small Acreage Farm Sales

For some products, an operator cannot generate much in sales on a small land base. Indeed, most SA farms generated very little, if any, farm production in 2007. Approximately 122,000 operations, or 42 percent of all SA farms, reported sales under $1,000 in 2007, compared with 31 percent of all farms.

Figure 3

**All farms and small acreage (SA) farms with $10,000 or more in sales in 2007, by operator age**

Percent of farms

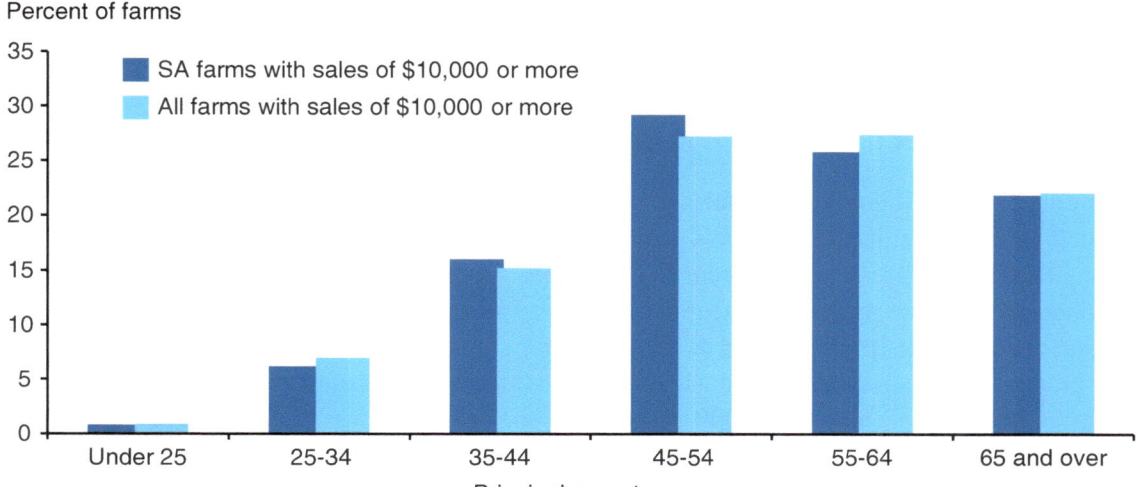

Number of farms = 294,000.
Source: USDA, Economic Research Service using data from U.S. Census of Agriculture, 2007.

Figure 4

**Small acreage (SA) farms with $10,000 or more in 2007, by sales category and operator age**

Number of farms (thousands)

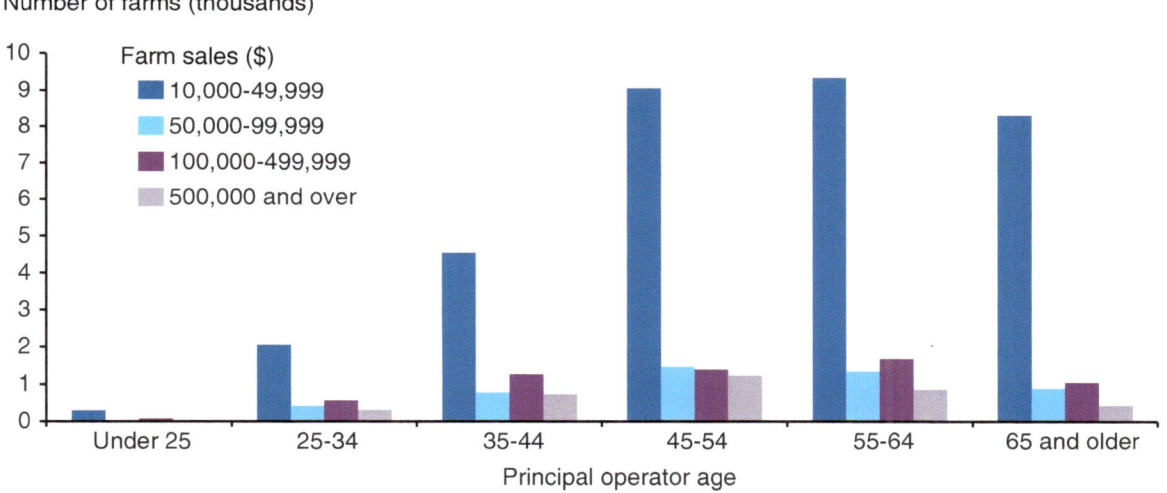

Source: USDA, Economic Research Service using data from U.S. Census of Agriculture, 2007.

Yet, approximately 50,000 (17 percent) SA farms reported sales of at least $10,000 in 2007 (see table 3), with 3,600 SA farms exceeding $500,000 in sales. To earn over $10,000 in gross sales in a given year, a farm operator has to commit significant resources to farming. For example, in 2007, a livestock farmer would need to have sold 22 feeder cattle at 500 pounds each, at the average 2007 price per animal of $462, to gross over $10,000. The time and effort needed to handle 22 feeder cattle is significant even on a part-time basis. An avocado producer in South Florida would need to sell more than 27,000 pounds of produce, requiring 3-5 acres of bearing trees at recent yields, to get a minimum of $10,000 in gross sales (Evans and Nalampang, 2012).

## Acres Operated by Small Acreage Farmers

A relatively high number of SA farms with $10,000 or more in sales in 2007 reported having 1, 5, and 10 acres (table 4), but survey respondents often round numbers in response to questions about acreage. In general, SA farms in this sales class are distributed fairly evenly by the number of acres operated.

## Farm Product Specializations and Sales of Small Acreage Farms

If one product or related group of products accounts for at least 50 percent of a farm's total value of production, it is identified as the farm's primary product specialization, according to the North American Industrial Classification System (NAICS) (see appendix table for more details). When a farm does not have one product or one related group of products that makes up 50 percent of the total value of production, it is classified as an "other crops" or "other livestock" operation. The NAICS product group labels are paired with corresponding sales estimates to identify the products of SA farms with annual sales of $10,000 or more, grouped by sales classes. Some SA farms had fairly high sales in 2007. Approximately 3,600 SA farms, or 7 percent of all SA farms, had sales of at least $500,000. SA farms with sales of $500,000 or more in 2007 averaged about $1.6 million in gross sales. SA farms in the intermediate sales classes (from $100,000 to $499,999) averaged roughly $200,000 in annual sales, and those with sales ranging from $50,000 to $99,999 averaged about $68,000. Not surprisingly, SA farms with $10,000 or more in sales accounted for most SA farm sales but just a small share of total SA farms (fig. 5).

The 46,000 SA farms with sales between $10,000 and $500,000 in 2007 were primarily active in floriculture, tree nurseries, and fruits and vegetables, while the 3,600 SA farms with at least $500,000 in sales were primarily active in confined livestock production. More than half of all SA farms specialized in three broad product groups—"other animals" (primarily horses), cattle, and fruit and tree nuts (fig. 6). However, these farm groups combined accounted for only one-fifth of SA

Table 4
**Small acreage (SA) farms compared to those with sales of $10,000 or more by acres operated, 2007**

| Acres operated | SA farms | SA farms with $10,000 or more in sales | Share of SA farms with $10,000 or more in sales |
|---|---|---|---|
| | *Number* | | *Percent* |
| 1 | 34,510 | 6,918 | 20 |
| 2 | 24,768 | 3,945 | 16 |
| 3 | 22,319 | 4,069 | 18 |
| 4 | 21,232 | 3,734 | 18 |
| 5 | 48,902 | 8,059 | 16 |
| 6 | 22,639 | 3,579 | 16 |
| 7 | 20,957 | 3,217 | 15 |
| 8 | 20,653 | 3,359 | 16 |
| 9 | 16,869 | 2,724 | 16 |
| 10 | 60,826 | 9,527 | 16 |
| Totals | 293,675 | 49,131 | 17 |

Source: USDA, Economic Research Service using data from U.S. Census of Agriculture, 2007.

Figure 5
**Small acreage (SA) farms by sales class in 2007**

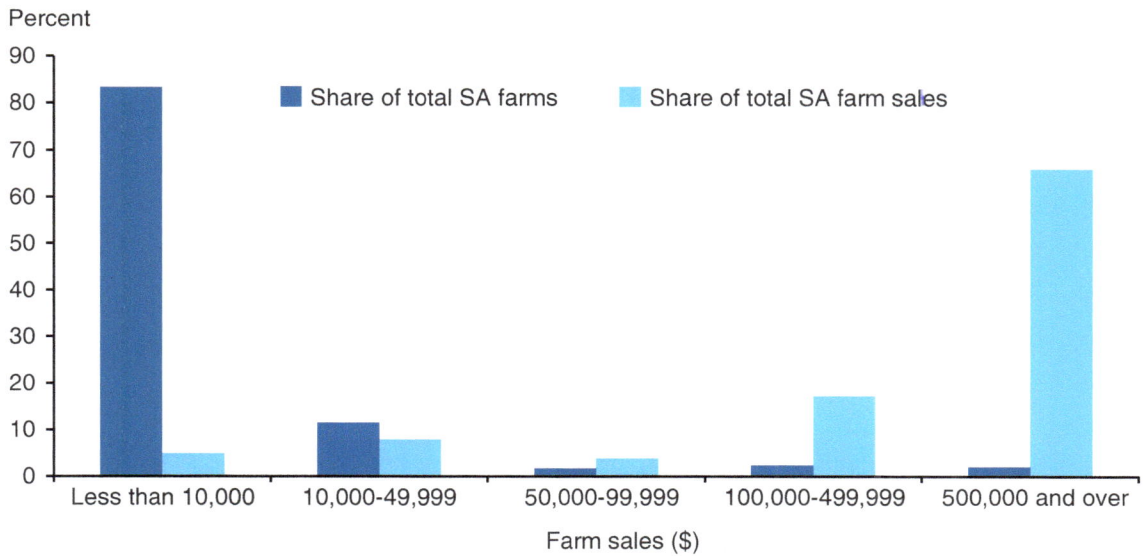

Percent

Source: USDA, Economic Research Service using data from U.S. Census of Agriculture, 2007.

Figure 6
**Small acreage (SA) farms and sales share by product specialization group, 2007**

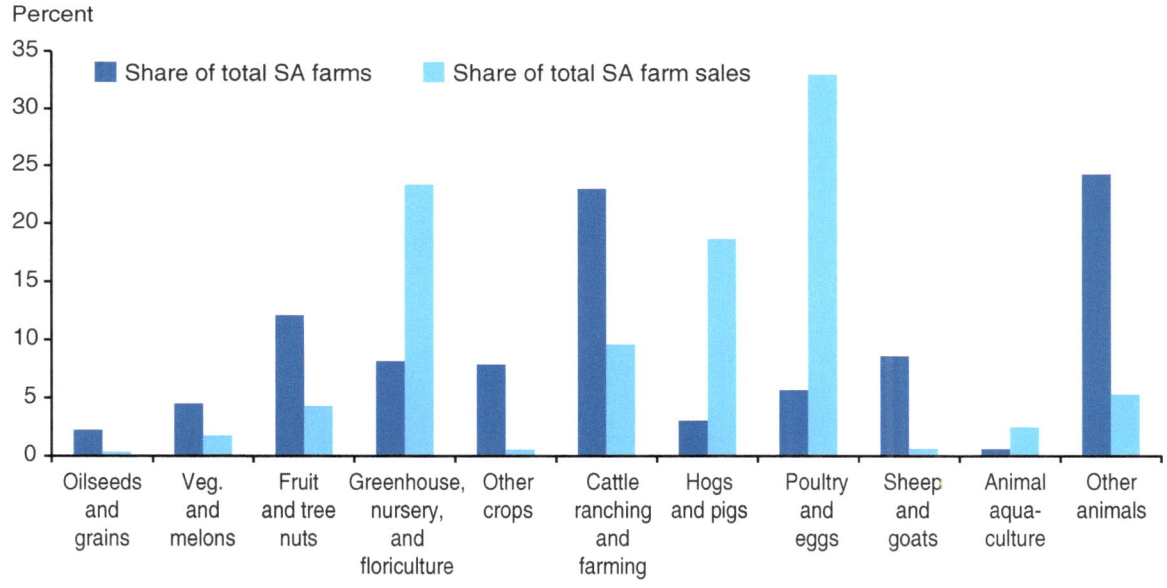

Percent

Sources: USDA, Economic Research Service using data from U.S. Census of Agriculture, 2007, and North American Industry Classification System.

sales in 2007. Most SA sales (75 percent) were in three other product groups—poultry and eggs, hogs and pigs, and greenhouse/nursery—though these products were produced on only 15 percent of SA farms. Farm counts and sales were low for SA farms producing grains and oilseeds—field crops that require acreage and input use not typically associated with small farms.

# Top-Ranking Small Acreage Farm Product Specializations by Sales Class

SA farms with $10,000 or more in sales specialize in a distinct set of farm products that varies with gross sales. For these farms, production does not always require extensive acreage, due in part to the production strategies used. Data on the top 10 products or groups of products produced by SA farms in various sales classes reveal several patterns, specifically the predominance of livestock, floriculture, and other specialty crop farms, particularly as sales increase (table 5; also see appendix table for a list of all SA products for each sales class).

Table 5
**Top 10 products for small acreage farms with sales of $10,000 or more in 2007, by sales class**

| Rank | Sales class ($) | | | |
| --- | --- | --- | --- | --- |
| | 10,000-49,999 | 50,000-99,999 | 100,000-499,999 | 500,000 (+) |
| | Farm count (sales - $ millions) | | | |
| 1 | Floriculture | Floriculture | Floriculture | Hog and pig farming |
| | 3,296 (77) | 1,097 (76) | 2,000 (421) | 909 (1437) |
| 2 | Beef cattle | Beef cattle | Nursery/Tree production | Poultry hatcheries |
| | 3,577 (72) | 559 (39) | 986 (195) | 110 (1,066) |
| 3 | Other noncitrus fruit | Nursery and tree production | Hog and pig farming | Broilers and other meat type chicken |
| | 3,502 (70) | 566 (38) | 738 (189) | 802 (1,014) |
| 4 | Other veg. (except potato) and melon | Other veg. (except potato) and melon | Broilers and other meat type chicken | Floriculture |
| | 3,451 (70) | 329 (22) | 457 (147) | 623 (695) |
| 5 | Nursery and tree | Horses/Other equine | Beef cattle | Chicken egg production |
| | 3,048 (65) | 307( 20) | 467 (100) | 164( 322) |
| 6 | Horses/Other equine | Hog and pig farming | Chicken egg | Turkey |
| | 3,223 (64) | 265 (19) | 337 (96) | 155 (237) |
| 7 | Orange groves | Other noncitrus fruit farming | Dairy cattle/ milk | Nursery and tree |
| | 1,717 (40) | 254 (16) | 305 (73) | 274 (276) |
| 8 | Grape vineyards | Apiculture (bee keeping/products) | Finfish farming and fish hatcheries | Mushroom |
| | 1,534 (32) | 186 (13) | 204 (45) | 50 (147) |
| 9 | Tree nut farming | Cattle feedlots | Apiculture | Cattle feedlots |
| | 1,342 (26) | 134 (10) | 239 (45) | 55 (128) |
| 10 | Apple orchards | Dairy cattle/Milk | Cattle feedlots | Dairy cattle/Milk |
| | 1,087 (23) | 138 (10) | 152 (35) | 105 (147) |

* See appendix table for detailed sales and farm counts by class for all commodities.

Source: USDA, Economic Research Service using data from U.S. Census of Agriculture, 2007, and North American Industry Classification System.

Floriculture and mushrooms are high-value specialty products (see box "Selected NAICS 2007 Definitions" for products referenced in this section). Floriculture production ranked number one in all SA sales classes except for the largest ($500,000 or more). Small-acreage floriculture farms can yield high sales because of their high-value products. In addition, floriculture products are often grown under cover (for example, in greenhouses or hoop houses), which allows intensive production over an extended growing season.

## Selected NAICS 2007 Definitions

*Apiculture* - establishments primarily engaged in raising bees. These establishments may collect and gather honey and/or sell queen bees, packages of bees, royal jelly, bees' wax, propolis, venom, and/or other bee products.

*Cattle feedlots* - establishments primarily engaged in feeding cattle for fattening. The category excludes establishments primarily engaged in operating stockyards for transportation and not buying, selling, or auctioning livestock.

*Chicken egg production* - establishments primarily engaged in raising chickens for egg production. The eggs produced may be for use as table eggs or hatching eggs.

*Floriculture* - establishments primarily engaged in growing and/or producing floriculture products (e.g., cut flowers and roses, cut cultivated greens, potted flowering and foliage plants, and flower seeds) under cover and in open fields.

*Finfish farming and fish hatcheries* - establishments primarily engaged in (1) raising finfish (e.g., catfish, trout, goldfish, tropical fish, and minnows) and/or (2) hatching fish of any kind.

*Horses and other equine production* - establishments primarily engaged in raising horses, mules, donkeys, and burros.

*Oilseed and grain farming* - establishments primarily engaged in (1) growing oilseeds, such as flaxseed and cottonseed, and/or grain crops, such as corn and soybeans, and/or (2) producing oilseeds and grain seeds. These crops have an annual life cycle and are typically grown in open fields. This category includes corn silage and grain silage. The 2007 Census of Agriculture classified government-payment only farms as "All Other Crop Farming" (Census of Agriculture, 2007).

*Other animal production* - establishments primarily engaged in raising animals and insects (except cattle, hogs and pigs, poultry, sheep and goats, and aquaculture) for sale or product production. These establishments are primarily engaged in raising bees, horses and other equines, or rabbits and other fur-bearing animals, or producing goods, such as honey and other bee products. Establishments primarily engaged in raising a combination of animals with no one animal or family of animals accounting for one-half of the establishment's agricultural production (i.e., value of animals for market) are included in this industry group.

--continued

## Selected NAICS 2007 Definitions--continued

*Other noncitrus fruit farming* - establishments primarily engaged in growing noncitrus fruits (except apples, grapes, berries, and fruit(s) and tree nut(s) combinations). The category includes apricot, avocado, banana, cactus fruit, cherry, coconut tree, coffee, fig, guava, kiwi, mango, nectarine, olive, papaya, passion fruit, peach, pear, persimmon, pineapple, plantain, plum, pomegranate, prickly pear, prune, and quince farming.

*Other vegetable (except potato) and melon farming* - establishments primarily engaged in one or more of the following: (1) growing melons and/or vegetables (except potatoes; dry peas; dry beans; field, silage, or seed corn; and sugar beets); (2) producing vegetable and/or melon seeds; and (3) growing vegetable and/or melon bedding plants.

*Nursery and tree production* - establishments primarily engaged in (1) growing nursery products, nursery stock, shrubbery, bulbs, fruit stock, and sod under cover or in open fields and/or (2) growing short-rotation woody trees with a growth and harvest cycle of 10 years or less for pulp or tree stock.

---

NAICS = North American Industry Classification System. For more information, see www. census.gov/cgi-bin/sssd/naics/naicsrch?chart_code=11&search=2007

Mushrooms, primarily grown under cover, ranked eighth among products grown by SA farms in the largest sales class in 2007. Mushroom production does not require extensive land; in fact, small-acreage mushroom farms accounted for about 32 percent of all U.S. mushroom farms in 2007 and grossed just over $156 million in sales—about 16 percent of the $985 million in total sales by U.S. mushroom producers (U.S. Census of Agriculture, 2007-Table 37).

Apiculture (beekeeping), aquaculture, and beef production stand out in the midsized $100,000-$499,999 and smaller sales categories. Bees can be kept on small acreages because bee colonies are contained in small, portable structures. Farm-raised catfish and other aquaculture are produced in ponds that do not require large amounts of land. As with SA livestock operations, the feed for fish is generally purchased or provided by the integrator/contractor.

Livestock dominated production among SA farms in the $500,000 or more sales class in 2007. SA livestock operations tend to be highly specialized single-stage producers. The animals are typically in confined feeding areas. Feed is produced offsite and is delivered to the farm by the integrator or parent company. All the animals produced under contract are returned to the parent company. Manure is also usually moved offsite and sold or shared with local farmers or the community.

Beef cattle in feedlots are also in the midsized and lower sales classes. Stockers may raise calves on seasonal pasture, but some farms feed calves from harvested forages in confined or semi-confined settings. In the latter case, some stocker farms use very little land if they confine the animals and rely on purchased forages.

SA farms in the $50,000-$99,999 sales class differ from the larger sales groups because they typically produce vegetables and melons, horses, and noncitrus fruit. The 2007 Census of Agriculture reported over 576,000 horse and pony farms in 2007. Just over 15 percent of these farms operated on 10 or fewer acres. About one-quarter of all horse and pony farms sold animals in 2007, compared with over 30 percent of SA farms specializing in horses and ponies. Horses and other equine animals are bought and sold for a variety of purposes, including farm work, breeding, and competitive and recreational riding (AHP, 2009-10). The census data account for riding stables and other equestrian recreational facilities that sell horses and operate like a farm (Offutt and Korb, 2006).

Noticeably absent from the two largest sales classes are SA farms producing "Other Noncitrus" fruit. Fruit in this category are produced seasonally and require seasonal labor and substantial initial capital investments, which could be problematic for many SA farm operators.

In summary, SA farms with sales of $10,000 or more in 2007 produced a broad array of products, including various livestock such as beef cattle, chickens, rabbits, horses, goats, and sheep. However, the majority of sales were primarily from specialized livestock operations with contracts via a parent company. SA farms also produced floriculture, nursery and tree products, and specialty products such as mushrooms, fish, shellfish, and bees and bee byproducts, such as honey. Because of land and equipment constraints, SA farms with sales of $10,000 or more in 2007 did not produce peanuts, rice, dry peas and beans, and oilseeds and other traditional field crops in combination.

## Small Acreage Farm Production and Farm Sector Changes

SA farm production is influenced by farm sector changes and the subsequent opportunities available to some small farmers because of the growing importance of production contracts in the livestock industry. Structural changes such as larger farm sizes, improved technologies, increased specialization, and vertical coordination between production stages have enabled some SA farmers to carve out profitable niches with certain products, particularly through the use of production contracts and other organizational arrangements. These changes apply to animal and specialty crop production.

Production contracts are widely used by SA farms that raise hogs, poultry, or replacement dairy heifers, and by fed-cattle operations. Most hog and broiler production is now done in specialized stages. Hog production can be sorted into four distinct stages—breeding and gestation, farrowing, nursery, and finishing. Females are bred and maintained during the first stage. Birth to weaning takes place in the farrowing stage. In the nursery stage, pigs are cared for immediately after weaning until they reach about 30-80 pounds, when they are sent to the finishing stage as feeder pigs. There, the animals are fed to a finishing or slaughter weight of 225-300 pounds (McBride and Key, 2013). Traditional hog farms, known as farrow-to-finish, engage in all four production stages and also raise much of their feed. While most specialized hog finishing operations today raise crops and, hence, have substantial acreage, many finishing operations and most operations that specialize in earlier production stages forego feed crop production for onfarm use and have limited land needs.

Traditional livestock operations use land to raise feed crops for their animals and often use additional land for grazing and pasture. They raise animals from birth until they are ready to be sold for meat. In contrast, specialized operations focus on a single stage of the production process, typically under a production contract. The production contract is an agreement between a farm operation and a firm (or integrator) that sets the terms for transfer of the products from the farm to the integrator or to the integrator's next production stage, such as raising pigs only from farrowing to weaning, feeding yearling cattle to slaughter weights, or raising broiler breeders for eggs to go to hatcheries (the chicks will then be raised for meat on other farms).

In each case, the animals are typically kept in enclosed areas such as open-air pens, if cattle, or in grower houses if broilers and hogs. SA livestock farms with sales of $10,000 or more in a given year often use contracts to link to a larger, more complex operation.

Broiler production complexes include hatcheries, processing plants, and feed mills that are typically owned by firms called integrators. The integrators contract with farmers to "grow out" chicks to market weight for meat, produce eggs for chick production in hatcheries, and raise replacement hens for egg production. The integrator provides contract growers with feed, chicks or hens, and veterinary services. Broiler operations almost always specialize in a single stage. While some are large, diversified crop and livestock operations with extensive acreage, small broiler operators may require only a limited land base for two to three broiler houses and storage facilities for feed and manure if the manure is removed from the operation for use elsewhere as fertilizer. Under production contracts, the contractor typically provides feed and young animals to farmers, who raise the animals and are paid a service fee. Because feed is typically produced offsite, animals are typically confined rather than grazed, and manure is removed from the site, single-stage livestock operations do not require much land (MacDonald and McBride, 2009).

Most dairy farms have crop acreage, but a few purchase all their feed. In that case, it is possible to run a dairy farm with less than 10 acres for cow housing, feed and manure storage, and milking facilities. As in other concentrated feeding operations with no cropland, the manure must eventually be removed for use elsewhere, including as a fertilizer and soil amendment on other farms.

Not all stages of livestock production are conducive to small acreage farming. Beef cattle production includes cow-calf, stocker, and fed-cattle stages. Cow-calf operations consist of a breeding herd, often including a small number of bulls. Most cow-calf operations are land intensive, with cow herds fed from grazing on extensive pasture and hay land. Stocker operations purchase weaned calves from cow-calf operations and raise them until they are moved to feedlots. Stockers may raise calves on seasonal pasture, but some operations feed calves from harvested forages in confined or semiconfined settings. Some stockers may therefore use very little land if they confine the animals and rely on purchased forages, but most use a considerable amount of land for pasture and for feed production.

On fed-cattle operations, feeder cattle are placed in pens with groups of like cattle where they are given grain and special concentrates until they reach a specific size and grade. Most feedlots purchase their feed instead of growing it, so they use land for pens and for feed storage and processing. Small feedlots, with a limited number of pens, need very little land.

# Small Acreage Farm Financial Performance

A farm's financial performance can be gauged by looking at its net farm income and rate of return on equity. This analysis uses data from USDA's 2007 Agricultural Resource Management Survey (ARMS) instead of the census data used elsewhere in this report. ARMS gathers complete financial information needed for measures of farm financial performance, which is unavailable in the census data.

Though small farms in general have negative net farm income, most SA farms with sales of $10,000 or more in 2007 had positive net farm income. Net farm income, however, does not give a complete picture of the profitability of a farm since the expense measure used includes only cash expenses and depreciation and omits the opportunity costs of unpaid farm labor and capital investments. In particular, these omissions can complicate comparisons of financial performance between large and small farms. Large farms are more likely to use hired labor and to incorporate and pay salaries to family members, each of which are recorded as cash expenses. Family labor in farms that are not incorporated does not generate a cash expense; as a result, labor tends to be recorded as an expense in large farms but not in small farms, and failure to recognize this distinction can give a misleading impression of financial performance.

Farmers can often earn money by working off the farm—that is the opportunity cost of the hours that they spend working on their farms. Unless a farm is incorporated and the farmer is paid a salary, the opportunity cost of farm labor is not included as an expense when net farm income is calculated. But more complete measures of farm financial performance are available that account for the costs of using farm operator and other unpaid labor.

The rate of return on equity—a commonly used profitability measure—is net farm income adjusted to account for unpaid labor costs relative to the equity or net worth (assets minus debts) of the farm (see box "Calculating Net Farm Income and Rate of Return on Equity"). It measures the gross rate of return on the farm's invested capital, after accounting for cash expenses and unpaid labor costs.

Average rates of return on equity for SA farms varied widely among sales classes in 2007. Typically, SA farms and all farms with sales of less than $100,000 had negative rates of return—their returns after cash expenses did not cover the opportunity costs of their operators' labor expended on the farm (table 6). Similarly, both types of farms with sales of $100,000 and over in 2007 had positive median rates of return, although SA farms in the $100,000-$499,999 sales class had a higher median rate of return on equity than did all farms in that size class. Given the negative rates of return on equity faced by many farmers, why do they continue to farm? Farmers may continue—despite low rates of return—if they have a positive net farm income and undervalue their labor and management time or if they derive noncurrent income benefits from their farms (eventual capital gains from holding the farm for years). Also, they may receive off-farm income that enables them to continue farming, even if their net farm income is negative.

## Calculating Net Farm Income and Rate of Return on Equity

Calculating net farm income:

Net farm income = Gross farm income – expenses

**Gross farm income**

- Sales of crops and livestock
- **Government payments**
- Other farm-related income (receipts from custom work, machine hire, grazing fees, production contract fees, etc.); change in inventories
- Value of commodities consumed on the farm
- Imputed rental value of the farmhouse

**Expenses**

- Cash operating expenses
- Depreciation
- In-kind benefits provided to employees

Calculating rate of return on equity:

Rate of return on equity =

100× [(net farm income - charge for operator and unpaid labor - charge for management) ÷ net worth]

The rate of return on equity is a commonly used profitability measure that compares net farm income with the net worth of the farm. In the case of unincorporated farms, net farm income is reduced to reflect the opportunity cost of management and of operator and unpaid labor (see MacDonald et al., 2007, for more information on estimating unpaid labor).

*Working the Land With 10 Acres: Small Acreage Farming in the United States, EIB-123*
Economic Research Service/USDA

Table 6

**Financial performance of small acreage (SA) and all farms with $10,000 or more in sales in 2007, by sales class**

| Item | Sales class ($) | | | | |
|------|-----------------|--|--|--|--|
| | 10,000 to 49,999 | 50,000 to 99,999 | 100,000 to 499,999 | 500,000 or more | All* |
| | *Number*<br>Total farms—family and nonfamily | | | | |
| SA farms | 15,347 | 3,752 | 5,492 | 2,547 | 226,704 |
| All farms | 397,864 | 148,300 | 244,670 | 119,733 | 2,196,791 |
| | *Percent*<br>Farms with positive total net farm income | | | | |
| SA farms | 64.2 | 76.7 | 81.9 | 64.7 | 52.9 |
| All farms | 66.7 | 74.9 | 81.2 | 83.5 | 62.8 |
| | *Rate of return on equity*<br>(excludes farms with no or negative equity) | | | | |
| Median-SA | -8.1 | -0.2 | 5.9 | 3.3 | -6.7 |
| Median-All | -2.5 | **1.0 | 1.5 | 6.7 | -2.5 |

*Includes estimates for farms with sales less than $10,000 that are not shown separately. All farms total is a sample estimate based on ARMS data and differs slightly from estimates for U.S. Census of Agriculture referenced in other tables; based on 871 observations. **Coefficient of Variation = (Standard Error/Estimate)*100 and is between 25.1 and 50. The coefficient of variation is defined as the standard error of the estimate divided by the estimate, expressed as a percentage. It can be viewed as a measure of statistical reliability of the estimate. Any estimate with a coefficient of variation of 25.1 percent or more is indicated in the tables and figures. Note, however, that estimates close to zero—fairly common among financial ratios—have high coefficients of variation because the denominator of the coefficient of variation is small. In such cases, it is misleading to consider the estimate as unreliable (Ahrendsen and Katchova, 2012).

Source: USDA, Economic Research Service using data from USDA's Agricultural Resource Management Survey (ARMS), 2007.

# Small Acreage Farm Operator Household Income

Most farm households receive substantial off-farm income from wage-and-salary jobs, self-employment, pensions or Social Security, dividends, interest, and rent. Combined, these off-farm income flows provide the primary source of income for households operating small farms (those with gross annual sales of less than $250,000), as a group. Only as the farm grows in size (as measured by annual sales) does income from the farm business (farm income, including income from miscellaneous farm-related activities,[2] minus expenses) typically add positively to total farm household income. For all U.S. farm households, median total household income was about $54,000 in 2007 (compared with approximately $50,200 for all U.S. households) (Hoppe et al., 2010). In comparison, the median farm household income for the principal operators of all SA farms was $51,670—less than the median for all farms but above that for all U.S. households. Though median incomes vary when comparing SA farms and all farms with sales of $10,000 or more in 2007, median SA farm household incomes were higher in all sales classes except the largest (table 7). Median household income among principal operators of the largest farms was more than twice as high as median household income among SA farms in the $10,000-49,999 sales class. Nonetheless, households operating SA farms in the $10,000-499,999 sales classes had median incomes substantially higher than those of all U.S. farm households with similar levels of farm sales. Households operating SA farms with sales of $10,000 or more are not, in general, low income by national standards.

---

[2] Other farm-related activities can include operating another farm, renting out farmland to another operator, and the sale of forest products.

Table 7

**Household income of small acreage (SA) and all farms with sales of $10,000 or more in 2007, by sales class**

| Item | Sales class ($) | | | | |
| --- | --- | --- | --- | --- | --- |
| | 10,000 to 49,999 | 50,000 to 99,999 | 100,000 to 499,999 | 500,000 or more | All* |
| | *Number* | | | | |
| Farm households—SA | 14,520 | 3,675 | 5,417 | **1,966 | 224,322 |
| All | 387,081 | 143,118 | 236,769 | 110,152 | 2,143,398 |
| | *Percent* | | | | |
| Distribution of farm households SA | 6.5 | 1.6 | 2.4 | 0.9 | 100 |
| All | 18.1 | 6.7 | 11.0 | 5.1 | 100 |
| | *Dollars per household or farm* | | | | |
| Median farm household income | | | | | |
| SA | 60,875 | 75,644 | 94,218 | **145,051 | 51,670 |
| All | 50,277 | 57,934 | 78,424 | 145,051 | 54,428 |
| Mean farm household income | | | | | |
| SA | 84,357 | *82,846 | **169,260 | 174,537 | 72,085 |
| All | 78,744 | 100,034 | 95,332 | 232,000 | 88,796 |
| | *Percent* | | | | |
| Median operator farm household income as share of median of all U.S. households (CPS) | | | | | |
| SA | 121.2 | **150.6 | **187.6 | 288.8 | 102.9 |
| All | 100.1 | 115.3 | 156.1 | 288.8 | 108.4 |

Median income of Current Population Survey (CPS) = $50,233. ARMS 2007 estimates possibly differ from other years because 2007 ARMS weights are calibrated to the 2007 Census of Agriculture. + includes estimates for farms with sales less than $10,000 that are not shown separately. Total households does not include counts of nonfamily farms. **Coefficient of Variation (CV) = (Standard Error/Estimate)*100. * indicates that CV is greater than 25 and less than or equal to 50. The coefficient of variation is defined as the standard error of the estimate divided by the estimate, expressed as a percentage. It can be viewed as a measure of statistical reliability of the estimate. Any estimate with a coefficient of variation of 25.1 percent or more is indicated in the tables and figures. Note, however, that estimates close to zero—fairly common among financial ratios—have high coefficients of variation because the denominator of the coefficient of variation is small. In such cases, it is misleading to consider the estimate as unreliable (Ahrendsen and Katzhova, 2012).

Source: USDA, Economic Research Service using data from USDA's Agricultural Resource Management Survey (ARMS), 2007; based on 871 households.

*Working the Land With 10 Acres: Small Acreage Farming in the United States, EIB-123*
Economic Research Service/USDA

# Conclusions and Implications

Farms can operate as viable businesses on small acreage, but much depends on farm product choices and strategies. Analysis of small acreage farms in this report shows that production strategies, such as contracting, play an important role in livestock production, enabling farmers to operate on limited acreage by specializing in a single production stage. A similar strategy also holds for some specialty crop production, such as floriculture.

SA farms with sales of $10,000 or more in a given year produce a broad array of livestock such as beef cattle, hogs and pigs, dairy, chickens, rabbits, horses, goats, and sheep. They also produce floriculture; nursery and tree products; and specialty products such as mushrooms, fish, shellfish, and bees/bee byproducts such as honey. SA farms of this size are not generally able to produce peanuts, rice, dry peas and beans, and other traditional field crops such as wheat as their primary activity because of the land and equipment needed to generate significant sales of such products.

Four of the top five specializations for SA farms (ranked by sales) are in livestock production, and the fifth is in floriculture. SA livestock operations typically produce under contracts with larger companies (referred to as contractors or integrators), with SA farmers being paid for raising animals provided by the contractor, often with feed and veterinary services provided by the contractor as well.

Despite a nationwide shift in agricultural production to larger farms, small acreage farms with sales of $10,000 or more in a given year are a significant part of the farm landscape. While the majority of small acreage farms do not appear to be operating viable farm businesses, those that do have applied specific production and marketing strategies to achieve at least a modest amount of annual sales, and some produce in excess of $500,000 worth of farm products annually on 10 acres or less.

# References

Ahearn, Mary. *Beginning Farmers and Ranchers at a Glance,* Economic Brief No. 22, U.S. Department of Agriculture, Economic Research Service, January 2013, www.ers.usda.gov/publications/eb-economic-brief/eb22.aspx

Ahrendsen, Bruce L., and Ani L. Katchova. "Financial Ratio Analysis Using ARMS Data," *Agricultural Finance Review*, Vol. 72, Issue 2, 2012, pp. 262-272, www.emeraldinsight.com/journals.htm?articleid=17044258&show=abstract

American Horse Publications (AHP). *Equine Industry Survey, Summary Statistics, 2009-2010*, 2010, www.americanhorsepubs.org/resources/AHP-Equine-Survey-Final.pdf

Cash, A. James, II. "Where's the Beef? Small Farms Produce Majority of Cattle," *Agricultural Outlook*, Issue 297, U.S. Department of Agriculture, Economic Research Service, December 2002, pp. 21-24, http://webarchives.cdlib.org/sw1610ws5g/http://www.ers.usda.gov/publications/agoutlook/Dec2002/ao297g.pdf

Evans, Edward A., and Sikavas Nalampang. "Sample Avocado Production Costs and Profitability Analysis for Florida," University of Florida Extension, 2012, www.edis.ifas.ufl.edu/fe837#

Fuglie, Keith O., James M. MacDonald, and Eldon Ball. *Productivity Growth in U.S. Agriculture*, Economic Brief No. 9, U.S. Department of Agriculture, Economic Research Service, September 2007, www.ers.usda.gov/media/201254/eb9_1_.pdf

Hoppe, Robert A., and David E. Banker. *Structure and Finances of U.S. Farms: Family Farm Report, 2010 Edition*, Economic Information Bulletin No. 66, U.S. Department of Agriculture, Economic Research Service, July 2010, www.ers.usda.gov/publications/eib-economic-information-bulletin/eib66.aspx

Hoppe, Robert A., and Penni Korb. *Characteristics of Women Farm Operators and Their Farms*, Economic Information Bulletin No. 111, U.S. Department of Agriculture, Economic Research Service, April 2013, www.ers.usda.gov/publications/eib-economic-information-bulletin/eib111.aspx

Hoppe, Robert A., James M. MacDonald, and Penni Korb. *Small Farms in the United States: Persistence Under Pressure,* Economic Information Bulletin No. 63, U.S. Department of Agriculture, Economic Research Service, February 2010, www.ers.usda.gov/publications/eib-economic-information-bulletin/eib63.aspx

Jerardo, Alberto. *2007 Floriculture and Nursery Crops Yearbook,* U.S. Department of Agriculture, Economic Research Service, Outlook Report No. FLO-2007, September 2007, http://webarchives.cdlib.org/sw1s17tt5t/http://ers.usda.gov/Publications/flo/2007/09Sep/FLO2007.pdf

MacDonald, James M. *The Economic Organization of U.S. Broiler Production*, Economic Information Bulletin No. 38, U.S. Department of Agriculture, Economic Research Service, June 2008, www.ers.usda.gov/publications/eib-economic-information-bulletin/eib38.aspx

MacDonald, James, and Penni Korb. *Agricultural Contracting Update: Contracts in 2008,* Economic Information Bulletin No. 72, U.S. Department of Agriculture, Economic Research

Service, February 2011, www.ers.usda.gov/publications/eib-economic-information-bulletin/eib72. aspx

MacDonald, James M., Erik J. O'Donoghue, William D. McBride, Richard F. Nehring, Carmen L. Sandretto, and Roberto Mosheim. *Profits, Costs, and the Changing Structure of Dairy Farming*, Economic Research Report No. 47, U.S. Department of Agriculture, Economic Research Service, September 2007, www.ers.usda.gov/media/188030/err47_1_.pdf

MacDonald, James M., Penni Korb, and Robert A. Hoppe. *Farm Size and the Organization of U.S. Crop Farming*, Economic Research Report No. 152, U.S. Department of Agriculture, Economic Research Service, August 2013, www.ers.usda.gov/publications/err-economic-research-report/ err152.aspx

McBride, William D., and Nigel Key. *U.S. Hog Production From 1992 to 2009: Technology, Restructuring, and Productivity Growth*, Economic Research Report No. 158, U.S. Department of Agriculture, Economic Research Service, October 2013, www.ers.usda.gov/publications/err-economic-research-report/err158.aspx

Nickerson, Cynthia, Mitch Morehart, Todd Kuethe, Jayson Beckman, Jennifer Ifft, and Ryan Williams. *Trends in U.S. Farmland Values and Ownership*, Economic Information Bulletin No. 92. U.S. Department of Agriculture, Economic Research Service, February 2012, www.ers.usda. gov/publications/eib-economic-information-bulletin/eib92.aspx

O'Donoghue, Eric J., Robert A. Hoppe, David E. Banker, and Penni Korb. *Exploring Alternative Farm Definitions: Implications for Agricultural Statistics and Program Eligibility*, Economic Information Bulletin No. 49, U.S. Department of Agriculture, Economic Research Service, March 2009, www.ers.usda.gov/publications/eib-economic-information-bulletin/eib49.aspx

O'Donoghue, Eric J., Robert A. Hoppe, David E. Banker, Robert Ebel, Keith O. Fuglie, Penni Korb, Michael Livingston, Cynthia Nickerson, and Carmen L. Sandretto. *The Changing Organization of U.S. Farming*, Economic Information Bulletin No. 88, U.S. Department of Agriculture, Economic Research Service, December 2011, www.ers.usda.gov/publications/eib-economic-information-bulletin/eib88.aspx

Offutt, Susan, and Penni Korb. "More Women Turning to Horse Farming," *Amber Waves*, Vol. 4, Issue 4, U.S. Department of Agriculture, Economic Research Service, September 2006, http://webarchives.cdlib.org/sw1vh5dg3r/http://www.ers.usda.gov/AmberWaves/September06/ DataFeature/)

Regents of the University of Minnesota. "Commercial Fruit Production in Minnesota," 2007, http:// fruit.cfans.umn.edu/apples/beforeyoustart.htm

U.S. Department of Agriculture, Agriculture Marketing Service. *National Fruit and Vegetable Retail Report, Summary*, Vol. VI, No. 29, pg. 3, July 20, 2012, www.ams.usda.gov/mnreports/ fvwretail.pdf

U.S. Department of Agriculture, Economic Research Service. "Agricultural Resource Management Survey (ARMS)," 2007, www.ers.usda.gov/data-products/arms-farm-financial-and-crop-production-practices.aspx

U.S. Department of Agriculture, Economic Research Service. "Farm Household Well-Being," updated: August 27, 2012, www.ers.usda.gov/topics/farm-economy/farm-household-well-being/glossary.aspx%23income#income

U.S. Department of Agriculture, Economic Research Service. "Farm Household Economic Well-Being: Glossary," 2013, www.ers.usda.gov/topics/farm-economy/farm-household-well-being/glossary.aspx

U.S. Department of Agriculture, Economic Research Service. *Livestock, Dairy, and Poultry Outlook*, Outlook Report No. LDP-M-154, April 18, 2007, www.ers.usda.gov/publications/ldp/2007/04Apr/LDPM154.pdf

U.S. Department of Agriculture, Economic Research Service. "Vegetables and Pulse Data-Mushroom Outlook Tables (M-5)," 2007, www.ers.usda.gov/data-products/vegetables-and-pulses-data/outlook-tables.aspx

U.S. Department of Agriculture, National Agricultural Statistics Service (NASS). *Farms, Land in Farms, and Livestock Operations, 2010 Summary*, February 2011, pp. 26-27, www.nass.usda.gov/Publications/Todays_Reports/reports/fnlo0211.pdf

U.S. Department of Agriculture, National Agricultural Statistics Service (NASS). "2007 Census of Agriculture, Volume 1, Chapter 1: U.S. National Level Data, 2009, Table 49, Selected Operator Characteristics for Principal, Second, and Third Operator: 2007."

U.S. Department of Agriculture, National Agricultural Statistics Service (NASS). "Small Farms Fact Sheet," www.agcensus.usda.gov/Publications/2007/Online_Highlights/Fact_Sheets/Farm_Numbers/small_farm.pdf

U.S. Department of Agriculture, National Agricultural Statistics Service (NASS). "Mushrooms, Greenhouse, Nursery, Floriculture Fact Sheet," www.agcensus.usda.gov/Publications/2007/Online_Highlights/Fact_Sheets/Production/nursery.pdf

U.S. Department of Agriculture, National Agricultural Statistics Service (NASS). "2007 Census of Agriculture," www.agcensus.usda.gov/Publications/2007/Full_Report/Volume_1,_Chapter_1_US/usintro.pdf

U.S. Department of Agriculture, National Agricultural Statistics Service (NASS). "United States Summary and State Data, Volume 1, Geographic Area Series, Part 51," various, www.agcensus.usda.gov/Publications/2007/Full_Report/usv1.pdf

U.S. Department of Agriculture, National Agricultural Statistics Service (NASS). "United States Summary and State Data, Volume 1, Table 37. Nursery, Greenhouse, Floriculture, Sod, Mushrooms, Vegetable Seeds, and Propagative Materials Grown for Sale: 2007 and 2002," www.agcensus.usda.gov/Publications/2007/Full_Report/Volume_1,_Chapter_1_US/st99_1_037_037.pdf

U.S. Department of Commerce, U.S. Census Bureau. North American Industrial Classification System (NAICS), 2007, www.census.gov/cgi-bin/sssd/naics/naicsrch?chart=2007

# Appendix

Appendix table
**Small acreage total farms and sales for all commodity groups by sales class, 2007**

| Commodity group | Less than $50,000 | | $50,000-$99,999 | | $100,000-$499,999 | | $500,000 and more | | All farms | |
|---|---|---|---|---|---|---|---|---|---|---|
| | Farm count | Annual sales | Farm count | Annual sales | Farm count | Annual sales | Farm count | Annual sales | Farm count | Annual sales |
| All other animal production | 10,290 | $27,111,384 | 117 | $5,251,240 | 89 | $16,511,606 | 47 | $114,738,895 | 10,543 | $163,613,125 |
| All other grain farming | 132 | $440,363 | None | None | 10 | $1,977,486 | D* | D* | D* | D* |
| All other miscellaneous crop farming | 6,986 | $7,490,869 | 22 | $1,461,175 | D* | D* | D* | D* | D* | D* |
| Apiculture | 3,714 | $21,262,773 | 186 | $13,093,230 | 239 | $44,785,968 | 15 | $10,703,836 | 4,154 | $89,845,807 |
| Apple orchards | 3,121 | $29,523,711 | 68 | $4,508,989 | 12 | $1,576,368 | None | None | D* | D* |
| Beef cattle ranching and farming | 60,085 | $165,340,716 | 559 | $38,616,906 | 467 | $99,601,230 | 108 | $112,680,917 | 61,219 | $416,239,769 |
| Berry (except strawberry) farming | 2,335 | $19,988,393 | 56 | $3,547,648 | 34 | $8,212,962 | D* | D* | D* | D* |
| Broilers and other meat type chicken production | 454 | $1,357,867 | 15 | $989,650 | 457 | $146,761,087 | 802 | $1,013,684,666 | 1,728 | $1,162,793,270 |
| Cattle feedlots | 3,882 | $23,236,305 | 134 | $9,998,076 | 152 | $34,948,785 | 55 | $127,954,241 | 4,223 | $196,137,407 |
| Chicken egg production | 11,084 | $14,311,098 | 35 | $2,592,765 | 337 | $96,267,347 | 164 | $321,892,509 | 11,620 | $435,063,719 |
| Citrus (except orange) groves | 1,686 | $18,380,636 | 46 | $2,950,558 | D* | D* | None | None | D* | D* |
| Corn farming | 3,626 | $11,865,217 | 36 | $2,691,448 | 27 | $4,526,490 | D* | D* | D* | D* |
| Cotton farming | 34 | $131,017 | None | None | None | None | None | None | D* | D* |
| Dairy cattle and milk production | 1,600 | $18,674,975 | 138 | $9,691,346 | 305 | $72,903,085 | 105 | $146,651,983 | 2,148 | $247,921,389 |
| Dry pea and bean farming | 12 | $30,349 | None | None | None | None | None | None | D* | D* |
| Finfish farming and fish hatcheries | 550 | $6,014,206 | 90 | $6,237,210 | 204 | $45,396,528 | 58 | $81,449,202 | 902 | $139,097,146 |
| Floriculture production | 7,396 | $93,549,258 | 1,097 | $76,077,013 | 2,000 | $420,905,875 | 623 | $694,632,740 | 11,116 | $1,285,164,886 |
| Fruit and tree nut combination farming | 312 | $1,276,620 | None | None | None | None | None | None | D* | D* |
| Fur-bearing animal and rabbit production | 984 | $3,337,743 | 23 | $1,588,223 | 48 | $11,225,753 | 16 | $13,279,233 | 1,071 | $29,430,952 |
| Goat farming | 13,595 | $19,967,305 | 36 | $2,579,832 | 25 | $5,179,120 | D* | D* | D* | D* |
| Grape vineyards | 4,491 | $42,087,097 | 131 | $8,794,918 | 30 | $4,023,894 | D* | D* | D* | D* |
| Hay farming | 14,842 | $24,350,112 | D* | D* | D* | D* | D* | D* | D* | D* |
| Hog and pig farming | 7,049 | $28,771,768 | 265 | $19,478,347 | 738 | $188,965,413 | 909 | $1,436,670,448 | 8,961 | $1,673,885,976 |

continued

Appendix table
**Small acreage total farms and sales for all commodity groups by sales class, 2007--continued**

| Commodity group | Less than $50,000 | | $50,000-$99,999 | | $100,000-$499,999 | | $500,000 and more | | All farms | |
|---|---|---|---|---|---|---|---|---|---|---|
| | Farm count | Annual sales | Farm count | Annual sales | Farm count | Annual sales | Farm count | Annual sales | Farm count | Annual sales |
| Horses and other equine production | 55,057 | $118,726,533 | 307 | $19,891,396 | 146 | $25,218,434 | 25 | $28,798,102 | 55,535 | $192,634,465 |
| Mushroom production | 57 | $705,831 | 11 | $857,413 | 32 | $7,615,725 | 50 | $147,233,420 | 150 | $156,412,389 |
| Nursery and tree production | 9,920 | $85,592,108 | 566 | $38,370,443 | 986 | $194,827,960 | 274 | $275,726,141 | 11,746 | $594,516,652 |
| Oilseed and grain combination farming | 27 | $73,362 | None | None | None | None | None | None | D* | D* |
| Orange groves | 3,477 | $46,745,758 | 125 | $8,033,347 | D* | D* | None | None | D* | D* |
| Other animal aquaculture | 66 | $1,066,146 | 11 | $680,119 | 26 | $4,540,303 | D* | D* | D* | D* |
| Other food crops grown under cover | 631 | $12,315,652 | 99 | $6,843,946 | 78 | $16,789,530 | 26 | $24,236,813 | 834 | $60,185,941 |
| Other noncitrus fruit farming | 11,812 | $99,419,293 | 254 | $16,222,594 | 48 | $6,635,390 | None | None | D* | D* |
| Other poultry production | 2,312 | $7,653,953 | 37 | $2,612,805 | 58 | $15,054,425 | 15 | $11,937,764 | 2,422 | $37,258,947 |
| Other vegetable (except potato) and melon farming | 12,599 | $104,056,165 | 329 | $21,548,609 | 93 | $16,399,466 | 16 | $16,536,147 | 13,037 | $158,540,387 |
| Peanut farming | 25 | $57,712 | None | None | None | None | None | None | D* | D* |
| Potato farming | 190 | $1,344,892 | None | None | None | None | None | None | D* | D* |
| Poultry hatcheries | 203 | $512,498 | D* | D* | 12 | $2,729,288 | 110 | $1,066,192,925 | D* | D* |
| Rice farming | 11 | $45,713 | None | None | None | None | None | None | 11 | $45,713 |
| Sheep farming | 11,436 | $17,971,381 | 17 | $1,184,344 | 12 | $3,111,934 | D* | D* | D* | D* |
| Shellfish farming | 531 | $7,304,615 | 82 | $5,643,643 | 90 | $17,796,364 | 25 | $36,553,126 | 728 | $67,297,748 |
| Soybean farming | 2,465 | $6,906,540 | D* | D* | D* | D* | None | None | D* | D* |
| Strawberry farming | 390 | $4,748,811 | 42 | $2,903,985 | 72 | $9,689,405 | None | None | D* | D* |
| Sugar beet farming | 20 | $104,295 | None | None | None | None | None | None | D* | D* |
| Sugarcane farming | 10 | $50,323 | None | None | None | None | None | None | D* | D* |
| Tobacco farming | 986 | $10,530,044 | 10 | $582,258 | D* | D* | None | None | D* | D* |
| Tree nut farming | 7,009 | $40,814,429 | 17 | $1,134,300 | 47 | $15,941,795 | None | None | D* | D* |
| Turkey production | 350 | $1,197,476 | D* | D* | None | None | 155 | $236,514,891 | D* | D* |
| Wheat production | 286 | $546,242 | None | None | None | None | None | None | D* | D* |

None=no data existed for this category. D*=disclosure restrictions apply.
Source: USDA, Economic Research Service using data from U.S. Census of Agriculture, 2007.

www.ingramcontent.com/pod-product-compliance
Lightning Source LLC
Chambersburg PA
CBHW050423180526
45159CB00005B/2390